To The People Who Appear In My Dreams

and other poems

Arka Roy Chowdhury

BookLeaf Publishing
India | USA | UK

Presentation by *BookLeaf Publishing*

Web: www.bookleafpub.com

E-mail: info@bookleafpub.com

ISBN: 9789357446389

First edition 2022

DEDICATION

Dedicated to my parents, Arun & Lina, in the memory of whom I rest my head at night.

ACKNOWLEDGE MENT

Thank you to Vik Feyago Sen for continued guidance, and cover design.
Thank you to Shijo George for his picture on the book cover titled, Fishing on a hill, Meghalaya.

PREFACE

All of our history is in peril. The birds on the wires of yesterday are stale, bones and blood. The father who crawled in his family home is missing his limbs, the mother who sang has lost her voice. Everyone is forgetting everything, we are running into new days, leaving behind our spiritual past. This is the urgency in my writing. For the future to understand the present, for the present to understand the past. . After the breakdowns, the quarrels, after thinking over things and believing, after all of the hate, someone would finally understand. Here in these words lies a truth, and so far, no one has claimed it. But many years from now, when little children are grown and devoid of innocence , when the finality of life is clearer than the day, then perhaps, these writings will mean something.

FORGETTING

We are destined to forget
cold bodies in the morgue,
nude lovers at daylight,
forget geometry, parallel lines,
a friendly face,
the hypothesis of our ideals at youth,
much more, every day,
day after day.
We might require new sentiments,
draw them on our faces, ,
ghosts of some other love
would cast shadows in twilight.

Borrow somebody else's nostalgia,
wedding photographs,
a loving grandmother,
letters of both love and hate,
each night I see a new anguish burn.
I tire my train of thought,
owing to transit tickets of places
I have never visited.
Or it could be a catastrophic
death of a dog,
a wounded belly, slayed heart,

little fingers of a lost child,
in pictures they always look so well.

ORPHANED
TENDERNESS

My tenderness is marooned without being able
to
touch an admirable body.
My reverence for love is as infinite
as the dark belly of the night.
Even though the weather is changing like it
always does,
I scrounge for loveliness, homeliness,
all along in a suffocating moroseness
that consumes the passage of time.
In our joints the hammers pound for a long
while,
all through the white night of the large moon.
In any case, all we do is search, and hope,
and wonder why white hair and wrinkles break
our hearts,
When did this begin?
Wasn't I altruistic?
Gave up my clothes on the floors, and lied down
next to my lover,
even though we always knew how things will
end,

quite lonesome, quite alright though,
we are accustomed, we enjoy longing.

Hurt, my tenderness is deeply hurt,
embalmed by a white cloud on a strange day,
all over the place, as disobedient as a teenager,
it has no hands to touch, no face to feel,
and nobody to come home to.
My pants are torn from grief,
and the old walls are rain-fed, covered in moss,
tenderness gnaws at my bones.

TO THE PEOPLE WHO APPEAR IN MY DREAMS

I see you sometimes
during early mornings,
you look somewhat like my father,
wear my mother's smile,
and yet I do not know you completely.
I saw the lot of you
swimming in my bedroom,
the dreary view of my home
light up sweet passions in me,
but even then, you are all strangers.
My dreams are tied to the bedpost,
you let them loose on me.
You sit at the dining table,
wash your hands at the sink,
though, most often you are nondescript,
howling into the orifices of the atmosphere.
When it rained for two whole days,
you thought it would be funny
to appear as my weeping father,

I wiped your teary eyes,
your beard melted in my palms.
Now then, which one of you is real,
the divine,
how often do you feel lonely?
I thank human subconsciousness
for its angelic trepidations,
I am sleeping alone tonight,
like most nights these days,
and at times I think of calling out to somebody,
but I realise none of you are real.

AN URGENT NOTICE

Urgently looking for a new home,
away from this old one,
away from the shadows of all the previous ones.
A new home without stale tragedies,
because these days
nothing feels good anymore.
In the new home everything will feel new,
new people will come
and greet me with their new faces,
one new painting on each new wall,
new floors where drunk
and passed out past midnight will be a new thing
to do,
new food and their new smells,
a whole new breakfast, new ways to make eggs,
new sounds from the floor above,
and a new woman,
who will think of me lovingly,
as I look at her body in my new bed.

LEAVING JULY

Now that yet another July is in the past,
mud stained pavements are looking for solace.
How must the lotus feel,
incomprehensibly staring at the sky,
trying to dissociate from the clouds,
as like all things,
it is trying to forget the rain.
How must the miracle sparrow
wake in sleepy mornings,
unnoticed, unafraid,
alive for another day.

The days are yet soft,
as if brushed by a painter's imagination,
a beauty lends itself to our forgiving
consciousness,
alarmed by the wetness on leaves,
the soft earth sinks our hearts inside it's cold
womb.
Where in the world are we headed;
into August, isn't it?
Where there will be no traces of July,
yet so much rain is due,
when countless yellow leaves
will be embedded on the pitch dark roads,

and we will walk over them.
Until the windows start to speak once more,
violently,
and we are so far away from our birth,
that the August sky, it's soot-like face
will settle on our roofs,
on our roads we will find its endless epitaphs.
All for nothing,
as we are only a flicker of light on the canvas of
this vast world,
unduly alive for a brief moment,
burdened with a heavy air
that collides against our skin,
and we rub off its traces with a strike of our
palm.
We forget so easily.

WATER HYACINTHS

A water hyacinth,
breeds inside my heart,
lovingly.
Though it is older than me,
older than the warm perseverance of the sun,
and I hold onto its stems,
partly drowned.
It is certain that my ten year old self
stands for an eternity,
facing a certain pond at dusk,
the smell of mud in the air,
my knees bleeding,
while I wonder if it is yet time to go home,
and what makes those cicadas roar in the wild?

EXALTED

See men and women who live in love,
see men and women who live.
See me. I am fastened to the floor.

You are wrong to think of me,
I am forbidding nostalgia from today.

Love is a thin stream.
It has no face. Nobody knows how often
you go away,
or when you return to it.
But it is true that when the water recedes,
it leaves you bewildered.

I have seen the Ajanta cave paintings
in pictures.
They are so unaware of me,
and yet I am longing for them, their stoic gaze,
I am devoting my heart to them as
my old loves are all fruitless.
I feel exalted.
I took birth inside the womb of that cave in my
dreams last night,
when a great heron was seen flying
outside in the open sky

ON SLEEPING WITH WOMEN

Sleeping with her,
sleeping beside her,
all sleeps are always the same,
In retrospect, quite demanding.
How must my hand be,
where should her head be buried,
on the chest, on the back, or just aloof?
What must be the conversations?
About old lovers,
about politics, and philosophies,
or the symptoms of a heart attack?
What will she think?
What does she like or dislike?
How often should we kiss,
with eyes closed or open?
Any thoughts on music?
I once had a moment with Chet Baker,
so not that, makes me think about it.
What if she likes Ravi Shankar?
Or has no thoughts about music at all?
What then?
Is smoking permitted? What if I burn the bed?

What then?
Her immense passion could be too much for me,
my alcoholism could be too much for her,
or the fact that we are really strangers,
and I will never know her first love,
and she will never find out about my fears.
Then in the morning, if she doesn't like my face
any longer,
I will wear my shoes and do a little dance for
her.
This already sounds quite horrible.

TO A GIRL WHO BURIED HER DEAD KITTEN

I haven't heard about your cat in a while,
I was thinking about her today,
and meant to ask you
whether she is still looking for her dead child.
If you are still saddened from all that,
and whether the rains in your city
are as unbearable as I imagine them to be.
Do you drop flowers at the grave
of the dead kitten in your backyard?
Do tiny fruits roll over its decaying body during
a storm?
Does it's little face come to your dreams?
If it was alive now, I bet you would be
busy, quite busy.
But I hear that now you are looking for
something,
as we all do from time to time;
or for someone.

Anything other than what we have going on in
our lives ,
anything other than the remembrance of days.
I am thinking of sending you a packet of cat
food, and some flowers,
for the cat and her dead kitten.
But this month has been hard,
I barely have any money for whiskey,
I don't think you would mind,
but if you do, then I apologize.
What else is there to say?
Oh,
I am thinking of going somewhere new,
and living in pretense for a few weeks.
I guess this is what is popularly known as
happiness.

THINKING ABOUT JALAPAHAR

In Jalapahar, your eyes are forgiven.
Truly, emancipation is due in these burning
mountains.
Long winged birds find treetops,
and the hills are moving closer to the sky.
On days when it rains on the top field,
you can stand afar and observe from a dry patch
of land, and look for someone to share the
serenity with.
Each morning
Mount Kanchenjunga is a cradle for the sun,
whose seemingly round head is a bonfire.
In Jalapahar you are with stinging nettles, dog
leaves, tiny beetles, and fluffy headed
dandelions.

Too many birds go missing in Jalapahar,
they lose their memory of home and run into
unidentified objects.
Too much is at stake here,

youth, innocence,
first loves ,
little pilgrimages to the main town that most
times end in haziness. .
Then 'round the bend of the old roads,
some evenings if you happen to bend your neck
to look up at the wondrous sky,
you see a moon that is only for you to see.
In Jalapahar, you aren't of your past,
you are born anew.

INHERITANCE

Everything is sad,
midnights in the city wear out,
turn into peculiar mornings,
and you blend into its chorus.

It is always the case.
Lord Curzon stands unannounced
for decades,
he has no place to go. I do understand that
sentiment.
Where would you go during such mornings?
To the river?
To the bakery for a slice of cake? The
crematorium?
Everything is infinitely sadder,
clouds frown upon Calcutta,
as does the windows that flip-flap in the wind,
and the buses that rush to the airport
are the buses that rush back
with ghoulish faces peering out from tiny seats.

Sadder; because being sad isn't enough,
what will the flowers think
if we half-heartedly sink our heads
into the corner of the bed,

and don't really burn our hands
in the tempest of our past.
What will our fathers say,
our fathers of Calcutta,
who disappeared from their ageing homes,
and now sit staring from their old walls,
who handed down this little sentiment that we
bear, unexplained.

PROOF OF LIFE

The sky shuts down in the evenings.
Dirt roads lie empty in twilight.
Birds gambol freely for a brief moment,
before vanishing from the telephone wires.
What a tremendous emptiness
wraps the body.
Those rays of light aslant,
they are the last of a great bickering
between human and nature.
Then someone from afar comes close.
Eyes adjust, warmth returns,
and you recognise yourself
on a stranger's face.
Reassurance. On a futile path we lay.
Alive.

JEREMY, AIZAWL

At midnight
as his eyes remain stitched,
the hills of Lushai stir a dream,
and into its cold wind he drowns.

He tells me that he makes his way
galloping through memories,
all the days tied to a strange satisfaction,
in midsummer, or at the end of December.
Nothing like you would imagine,
not the least common,
but honest, and grand,
magnificent like the surrounding hills that
know his faults.
There is a sense of where the heartaches hang,
where he sang a hundred songs in pain.
Then after running a paintbrush through a broad
canvas,
he wept at its merciful feet in a remembrance.

So now he says -
When the clouds moved away,
I began to awake,
and my eyes hurt from the light, elated.

Life, how beautiful are its secrets,
in its vestibule I find my past lying in the sun,
waiting for an entry,
so I can lead them into my generous fate.
Can't you hear? Lushai sings for me.

A CIGARETTE

Late last night,
when I turned to the pack of cigarettes,
I found just three of them, innocently unaware of
tragedy.
As I know that sometime during the windy night
as I grab hold of the pack,
and find none inside,
everything will begin to fall apart,
and the cold wind will burn my skin.
I will start rummaging through the drawers,
my father's unused cupboard,
and unknowingly my eyes will warm up, and I
will feel a betrayal.
Don't you feel it too?
As everything leaves you to your solitary self,
your life depends on a single cigarette.

GOD IN CALCUTTA

I have not heard God crying, not yet.
I am human, my ears are still vacant.
When will you come home? Will you drink tea?
Sit down for a while please,
and afterwards you can break down into tears.
Fill the void of my home with your tears,
you have a lot of sins on your shoulders, I know
you do.
I still go to the market,
with a bag under my armpit, cigarette on my
lips,
I leave behind all the dirt and walk ahead.
I still drink tea by the old roads in Calcutta,
and think of going to the airport
to see people go away from all this dreadfulness.
Calcutta today is a massive graveyard.
At noon, I yearn for night, at night, I yearn for
day.
I think maybe tonight you will finally appear,
and tell me that you feel sad for me,
I feel sad for you too.
You are unable to smile.

You are hopping from tram to bus,
lost in the crowds of Sealdah,
looking for even a semblance of your image.
There are no birds in your blue sky,
Calcutta is threateningly dull for you.
You are alone, tired, can't even cry anymore,
I have no thoughts.
But to hell with everything,
let the sun burn the city down,
we will walk into the river.
The water is not as cold these days,
it is swelling up with rain.
Everything will become one, you will see, it has
to,
you will become God once again.

A FAMINE

I refute pale sentiments,
and exchange them at the supermarket
for lonely pigeons that gather outside,
who once knew me,
and nested in my mind,
but have now flown away.
In a perennial hunger for art, or love,
or something that can delude me into thinking
that this after all is my fate (and that will do just
fine),
I wear my dead father's shirt, and try to map his
face in the mirror.
This hunger is an incremental scheme,
vegetables do no justice to it, meat, rice, milk,
they are worthless.
Women, I eat their tragedies with my mouth,
but nothing feels right.
So upon learning about this catastrophe, I try
uncovering the meaning of the sky,
to decide whether Eugene Boudin was really
serious about its colours.
With hunger in its abundance,
as an irrational country lunatic,
I watch a great storm pass through my home,
beating down all sentiments of nature,

and some tall trees gather some courage
to lovingly feed me a few sacrificial leaves.

29

WHERE THE RUNNER GOES

Fault lines on the forehead,
when the runner bends over to light a cigarette,
or when in the bus/train/aeroplane,
the sun looks into the eyes.
Lying in bed, unable to think,
there is also not much to say,
Thank god for darkness,
the birds tend to shut up,
people tend to grow louder,
and the runner paves new ways to forget.
In a rocket bus,
the long-distance with open wounds,
searching for time,
the charisma of moonlight
dissuades all reasons. Blinded -
there is no need for love,
not that again.
Always catching you unaware,
the runner can get up and disappear
for endless days, on a fiery asphalt that is
eternal.
No one follows

where the runner goes,
onto someone else's desolation,
as a spectator who
having completed the odyssey,
is only there to see.

WHAT THE RAINS BRING HOME

It's raining like it always does,
muddy roads, troubled birds,
and the disclosure of memories,
are some of its trapping that
we ought to live with,
once again this time.

The boats must be hitting
against the shores of the Ganges,
but there is no one to witness it,
everybody is dealing with wet window panes,
slowly lifting their eyes
to see how hard it rains.
When will it stop?
What could have possibly gone wrong?

God has no answer to give,
there is just so much misery in his mind,

God is in solitude,
and we are so alike in the rain.
I am remembering sunlight,
and comforting my beating heart,
silently, sitting still on a chair,
smoking, thinking,
everything will be alright,
we will once again return to our balconies
to hang the clothes to dry,
smile at our neighbours,
take a picture of the city outside our homes.
Then maybe I can take a nap,
and upon waking,
find some of the people
who had once disappeared from earth,
standing by the bed,
their bodies all wet,
they had forgotten their umbrellas back home.
Then as they wipe themselves dry,
and sneeze into the towels,
I can put a saucepan up for tea.
Wouldn't that be something?

OUTSIDE

The day never ends sooner,
I, with my aggrieved memories
riding on a rickshaw
through familiar neighbourhoods,
find time for lacklustre passions.
Erasing the city of my birth,
slowly erasing pain,
and love,
both, together,
as they seem to be in bed,
this fragile mind
may get a chance to weep.
Those lonely clouds move
in the opposite direction
to the moving bus,
and also to you
who waited for the bus at a street corner

to move towards somebody.
Each time I see those clouds
they see me too,
arriving at conclusions
at dawn,
or sometimes even before the light
falls on a sleeping child,

and its mother dreams of
her own father and his helpless face
at the hour of death.
I guess I am deeply unaware
of my empty hands,
as I grip the rickshaw at every bumper on the
road,
 a heaviness in my palm,
feeling sufficient for now.

LOVE

At last, a love poem.
2:43 am, all the dark skies are in meditation.
Now think of love, or forgiveness.
It is one and the same.

Rows of recurring loves,
catastrophic loves, unending loves,
love of art, sexuality,
in love with you,
like sugar after bitter medicine,
like morphine for cancer.
In love with somebody
because the moon also rises,
sometimes, at the end of day,
so you think of lips,
shadows, bare legs.
You think why must I love?
Why must I be born
in someone else's arms,
why must I say things
that doesn't sound too good on my lips?
In love with you,
like the memory of Kanchenjunga in the mist,
sliding the curtains open throughout the day,
hoping for a glimpse.

Little Faith

You must have a little faith
in the white overalls of the doctor,
promises of rain, sun,
Henri Matisse's little lilies;
whatever you can hold on to.
A little faith in Begum Akhtar's laments,
in the China Town baos,
even though you are worried sick at 5 am,
looking for the closest bed to crash.
A little faith in the hair band of a dead mother,
in the weather forecast,
a tiny bit of faith in the statue of Tagore,
who for all good reasons, reminds you of
innocence.
We can't go on living like this,
we must gather courage for some faith.
A little faith is what kittens have
when they show up at doorsteps in Calcutta.
Have a little faith in the past,
in the old grandfather, and the father before him
who once killed a snake.
A little faith in friends, and their friends
who show up on Sundays to bleed at hospitals.
In lovers or even those who refused to be loved,
in the warmth of winter Sun that burns the back,

in the workers who are creating mega homes,
a parrot whom you have taught all your
favourite words.
Have a little faith,
for everything else is ready to go into darkness,
everything else can always fail,
except for the faith you carry,
your children will see it in your eyes and say.
my father was a kind man,
my mother was always so hopeful.
It will break them down, but they will live.
It will be fine.

www.ingramcontent.com/pod-product-compliance
Lightning Source LLC
LaVergne TN
LVHW010918200726
843509LV00013B/1985